urpose

# *FOOTSTEPS IN THE SAND*

Edited by

Neil Day

First published in Great Britain in 2001 by
TRIUMPH HOUSE
Remus House,
Coltsfoot Drive,
Peterborough, PE2 9JX
Telephone (01733) 898102



HB ISBN 1 86161 824 7
SB ISBN 1 86161 829 8

# *FOREWORD*

Imagine you were trapped on a tiny island with no company, barely any food and a lack of shelter from the scorching heat of the sun above. You have with you the means to write one last message to the world before placing it in a bottle and hurling your last chance of contact into the sea. But what message would you write? The poets within this anthology have all written and share their own final thoughts to the people they know. Some have a special message for their loved ones, whilst others tell of how they long to be rescued and what home comforts they truly miss.

Together they make for a serious, funny and often romantic collection of poems, all calling out to be heard.

Neil Day
Editor

# *CONTENTS*

## Without You

Without words I can speak the truth,
and with truth you can save my soul.
Too many values to uphold -
- enough to fill the deepest hole.

Without love I could live so well,
and being well we could do much more.
Too many lie sick in their love -
- enough to fight and go to war.

Without an image I am free,
and I'd be free to be with you.
Too long I've been trapped in this shell -
- enough to know my love is true.

Without rules I would be so bright,
and being so bright I'd be a star.
Too bright to hide out in the dark,
but bright enough to shine so far.

Without you I am nothing, lost,
and when lost, I'd never be found.
Too far gone for you to search -
and so I wander, underground.

***Natasha Doras***

## Eternal Love?

Years have passed, but still I miss you
I hope you are missing me too
I do my best to get on with life
While you are sleeping with your new wife.

Your words were harsh and hateful too
But that's not how I remember you.
I remember your eyes and friendly smile
That said, 'Come over and stay a while.'

And so I did, but you hurt my soul
Now in my heart you've left a hole.
No one can ever replace you, it's true
But I'll try to find a life that is new.

Now your love is all too rare
But I always wonder if you still care
Of all the time we spend apart
Your love will never leave my heart.

***Julie D Coventry***

## Me!

I smile in all recognition,
Of things I have done in the past,
Idly making decisions,
That sometimes were made to last.

Of dreams that became reality,
Some that have still stayed a dream,
Visions some ugly, some pretty,
Some that are hard to believe,

But my past is done and over,
With hardly any regrets,
Experiences I have been through,
Are ones I will never forget,

One day I will write my life down,
For all who care to see,
As then my ode will be longer,
A whole book I'll write about me!

***Jacqueline Emma Aldridge***

## OUTSIDE WORLD

Dear potential rescuer

I often longed for some time alone
A little space to call my own
But I didn't quite plan it this way

My food sources are rather meagre
I must confess that I am eager
For caffeine and a box of Belgian chocolates

The sun has tanned my legs at last
Though the heat has me fading fast
What I wouldn't give for a bottle of factor 10

Tell work I won't be back on Monday
Oh, and give my love to all and sundry
This is not a time to bear grudges anymore

When you'll get this, God only knows
How will you find my words in prose?
As a last note I hope you'll find it quite witty

I never wanted to be an unsocial bore
Liked to discover places I'd never been before
Yet this wasn't quite what I had in mind

So I'll say cheerio and hope and pray
You receive this tomorrow, if not today
As I'm getting a bit fed up with building sandcastles

PS. I haven't found one palm tree on this island.

***Nikky Braithwaite***

## STRANDED!

*Then* I awoke! The sea lapping at my side
Seagulls screaming above me
Bright sunlight blurring my vision,
My ship now lost! I find myself
Trapped on this tiny oasis?

*Alone!* So alone I am! No human form to be seen?
The only sound a rumble like thunder
From my starving belly!
My mouth parched like the sun bleached sand.

*Suddenly!* I see something bobbing!
Glinting in the ocean?
So I rush forward splashing against the waves!
To find a bottle! A corked bottle!
Dry I drink the dregs of some mulled wine.

*Then!* I sit and write you this?
'Please! Kind sir remember me!
On this here island in vastest sea!
Time will soon run quick and short,
If not soon a fish is caught!
On this island there is no tap!
So hurry soon if you find my map!

***James Ellis***

## A Super Idea

We thought what a super idea
A note in a bottle to see
If we threw it
Far out in the ocean
Would it reach some one
Across the sea
Well my brother and I love exploring
Gather shells or the odd
Coloured glass
And we put them in pots
Out in our garden shed
Over years we have gathered a lot
We like holidays better than school days
So we thought this note told you a lot
Mum and Dad said we could arrange to meet
If you find this, then do get in touch
I hope it's not floating forever
This note in a bottle has been
One of the greatest things we've ever done
As we watch it float out to the sea.

***Jeanette Gaffney***

## Rather Laboured This Message In A Bottle

Tony Blair!

What can one say
          or do?

I bet,
   both you and I,
          wish

He was on this island
          *alone!*

Instead of me.

***David Robinson***

## JETTISONED

'Of late strong feelings flowed 'tween us,
But now I leave you here like this.'
Calm words I cannot understand,
That none can fully comprehend.
To sit and hold my hand in yours
And pick at the dam that may pour forth
The torrents of a ruined heart
To drown you, if it will, ere part.
And here you sit with steady eyes
That gaze at mine and tell no lies;
And if I blame you that is sad,
But he deserves it who is bad.
And so you sit in front of me
Tearing out this soul from me.

My eyes are dry, my voice is clear,
And I am speaking, saying, 'Dear,
Although we'd only just begun
You leave me now. But it was fun.'

***Nina Havers***

## WHO DARES WINS

'Though I'm forced on this isle to die
Because no craft ever passed by
May this bottled advice have worth
As my last gift to those on earth:

It's surprising what you can do
To help your hopes and dreams come true
Allow the heart's powerful force
To lead you to the wisest course.

Live here in the now - don't harp back
Along the past's old worn out track
Take time to relax - slow the pace
Life should not be a hectic race.

For sure there may be a few tears
As you trip, sometimes on your fears
But angels are there by your side
To uplift when hope starts to slide

When worrying thoughts fill with dread
Use 'positive thinking' instead
Rise above each inhibition
By trusting your intuition.

We know not what good life may send
Or what lies around the next bend
Be brave - that's where success begins
In the end it's 'who dares' that wins.

***Tina Lipman***

## Rapped In A Bottle

*(Cry for help from a marooned rugby league fan on match day)*

Marooned on this deserted cay
I send by bottle this 'Mayday'!
Much as I would like to say
That I'll attend the match today;
Unless a rescue comes my way
I'll have no choice, I'm here to stay!
I trust that Salford will display
Their utmost talent in this fray.
Two points are due to come their way
If only they're not thrown away.
It never happened in their heyday
But lately they've begun to stray.
Now's time to come to grips and *play*,
Wipe Bradford off the pitch today!
Best wishes, Salford, anyway,
Just keep that Bradford bunch at bay!
Of course I'm sure there is no way
This bottle reaches you today.
I hope you've taped the whole game's play
For my eventual assay!
If you get this, and I'm still at bay,
Send a search party straight away!
They'll find this isle in Morecambe Bay.
Believe me, it's no holiday,
I'm cold and hungry, and have no way
To shelter from the constant spray!
Send help at once, or else this may
Have been the last time I've seen Salford play!

***Christopher Head***

## Lacking Bottle

This message is sent for anyone to find,
Anyone who would be so kind
As to pick me up and take me back,
To the homely comforts that I lack.

I'd first like to say that this isn't a laugh,
It's been weeks since I've had a bath,
Water everywhere and not a drop to drink,
That's not as funny as you might think.

If it wasn't for insects this place might be great,
But my hair's never been in such a state,
I've broken my nails and have no face cream,
Good job there's no mirror to make me scream.

The choice of diet is pretty drastic,
Right now I could eat a burger out of plastic,
I wouldn't go as far as to say a horse,
But caviar and chips would suffice of course.

I've emptied this bottle so that I could write,
To ask for help from my terrible plight,
I've drunk all the vodka so this better float,
I'm writing on the lining of my mink coat.

I'll pay the bill so don't hang about,
Just get me rescued and there is no doubt,
You'll get a reward, a pat on the back,
Just get me back to the bottles I lack.

***A T Giddings***

## Voyage To Somewhere

I carry a cargo of hope friend:
Sealed by the hand of a child:
Then thrown to the whims of the ocean
To ride cruel waves high and wild:
I've been nosed by seals and blue dolphins:
Lain long on warm golden sand:
Then snatched by the waves to continue
My quest to be found as planned:
I've hit jagged rocks without breaking:
'Cause luck sails with me each day:
For she knows the message I carry:
The heartfelt fears it does say:
So pray keep a watchful eye for me;
I once held sherry so dry:
Uncork me, and read each word clearly:
Then post your caring reply:
If luck left I'd surely be scuppered:
For here comes a mighty whale:
I once conquered space as one surfaced,
When hit for six by his tail.

***Violet M Corlett***

## MESSAGE IN A BOTTLE

When the first chink of light hit the trees
I began my quest.
Time was precious and the implications vast.
The waves crashed down against the rocks,
Shifting layers of sand and shingle.
Changing the momentum and the structure.
Moving timelessly on as I sat silent
Watching, waiting, wondering,
What difference could one man make,
Against the force of nature?
Why should I try?
Birds hovered overhead, calling to each other.
Swooping down and resting momentarily upon the waves.
A lone seal surfaced, chasing breakers on the horizon.
For the first time in my life, I prayed.
Was I really *'the only one'*?
I tried to recall my boy scout days and failed miserably.
What good was a tin opener without a tin?
I struggled to unleash the cork.
With nails desecrated by hours of gnawing and wondering.
Finally it shot its bolt and I rushed to retrieve it.
Feeling panic, fearing loss,
The paper nestling in its midst I returned it to its final resting place.
No turning back now.
I hurled it with all my might into the sea.
The message short but to the point.
*Will you marry me?*

***Janice L Williams***

## LOVE USES INDELIBLE INK

My dear precious ones
Will I ever see your beautiful faces
Smiling at me again?
Will I ever feel your loving arms around me?
What a fool I've been!
I've taken you for granted.
If only I could turn the clock back!

I would treasure your value
And laugh at your childish ways.
I'd spend less time on me
And more on you
- Laughing and loving
- Sharing your thoughts
And being your friend.
Forgive me.

I am on a desert island.
I may never be found.
But God is with me
May he protect and bless you
Till we meet again.
Our love for you is eternal
Your names are written
On the palms of God's hand.
He always uses indelible ink.

***Linda Fawkes***

## Island Of Nightmares

I went to France on business
Six months ago, or more
I hope it won't be very long
Before I stand outside our door
I miss my creature comforts
Most of all my bed
I hope to goodness this note arrives
I'm sure you thought I was dead.

I remember catching the ferry
And going to the bar - like you do!
I was on the homeward stretch
Coming home to you
I remember getting drunk in the ship's bar
I need anaesthetic on the high sea
It stops me getting queasy
Though it makes me go weak at the knee.

I must have lost my balance
And wobbled overboard
I don't think anyone noticed
If they did I was totally ignored
I got washed up on this island
There's a few trees and a fisherman's shed
I'm not much of a survivor
It's ages since I've been fed.

I dream of stew and dumplings
And mouth-watering apple pie
If I'm not rescued shortly
It will all just be 'Pie in the sky'.

***Anthony Gibson***

## WRAPPED INSIDE

A present wrapped in memories
Of joy and hurt and love,
I cannot send it to you -
No post goes up above.
Your twenty-first is special,
Though you're not here with me,
I pray you're up in Heaven
With Jesus and Mary.
I miss you and I love you,
Please pray for me today,
Have a lovely birthday son,
That's what I want to say.
In my mind's eye I can see you
Smiling from above,
Just gently touch my shoulder,
I'm yearning now your love,
Your presence deep inside my heart,
To sing your song I'll try
Beside your lovely resting place,
My son - my golden boy.

***Phil Robinson***

## DESERTED ISLE

What a blessing I have pen and paper to say,
I hope you'll receive this message one day.
You must be wondering where I am,
I decided to voyage with my friend Sam.
We were on a ship but it sank near these isles,
There's not a soul around for miles and miles
Sam must've drowned, but I swam to the shore
I've cried and prayed for a month or more.
I'm living on fruit I found on the trees,
And at night alone, I listen to the breeze.
I know God is with me and one day I'll see,
His glorious face through eternity.
But meanwhile I'm missing your faces around,
Hearing your footsteps upon the ground.
I've been rather alone through all the years,
But have had friends to share the smiles and tears.
There's not a ship or a plane in sight,
But I feel God's presence with all His might.
If He was not with me I'm sure I'd go mad,
For at times I feel so lonely and sad.
I can see some birds all flying so free,
But they have each other for company.
As I write this note, I feel so alone,
How I wish I could reach someone by phone.
Only God knows if you'll receive my plea,
To come to this island and rescue me.
If you should get this note, please do your best,
To find this island - somewhere in the west.
Meanwhile I will continue to pray,
As I watch the sea day after day,
Hoping and praying a ship will draw near,
To take me back home, so precious, so dear.

***Nicky Young***

## SUNDERLAND HARBOUR 1864

*(Inspired by a painting by John Wilson Carmicheal 1800 to 1868)*

Navy blue horizons with lightning
Silhouetted across a grey starlit sky,
Sea storm raging a ship in turmoil
Lifeboats bouncing, rolling, fearsome from capped waves
Endless terror on the faces of the crew
As oars flash and twist through frozen white salt crusted hands
Panic and horror as two boats collide
Poor souls dead before they hit the icy water
The main mast splits at the deck
Pirouetting down to seal the fate of another lifeboat
Half lowered over the leeward side
Twenty men officers and the captain
The last boat to leave the stricken 'Jack Tar'
As the harbour rock split her hull in two.

***Douglas Bonthron***

## WISH YOU WERE HERE (MAROONED)

On this alien shore I was blown
And I wish you were here,
For I never feel alone
And anywhere is always home,
When you are near.

You, could be anyone
Young, old, male or female,
Each day I've been gone
I pray and I long
That today is the day I see your sail.

***Keith Tissington***

## SHIPWRECKED

My hopes sail out with that bottle
As the tide sweeps it away from the shore
Bearing the message and my plea for help
While I curse my fondness to explore

This island had looked so inviting
With sighing palms and fine golden sands
But the treacherous reef that wrecked my boat
Shipwrecked me miles from the nearest mainland

There's not a soul I can find that lives here
And fresh waters in such short supply
There's no food and in days I'll be starving
If help doesn't come soon I will die

The summer sun mercilessly beats down
There's no escape from the glare and the heat
With no cave or thicket to shield me
I have blisters on hands, face and feet

Will my love back home be thinking of me
Or has she dismissed thoughts of me from her mind
Since I stormed away from her in my temper
But then again, they say that love is blind

Perhaps when I'm finally rescued
She'll forgive and say she still loves me
And lay on for me a sumptuous feast
To show that our love is as it used to be

But two weeks have passed since my shipwreck
And it looks like I'll never be found
My strength is fading, I sense the end is near
But wait! What's that strange throbbing sound?

***Don Woods***

## Thoughts On Hold

I'm putting my thoughts of you on hold.
It may seem hard, it may seem cold
But there's a life outside of you,
And other things that I must do.

No longer will I sit and dream
Of the when, the where, the might have been,
The you and me that cannot be,
Or wishing one and one made three.

Those conversations in my head
Are really better left unsaid.
It's much, much wiser to forget
Than think and dream, and then regret.

***Joyce Walker***

## THE DESERTED

The waste bank should have claimed this glass.
Perhaps I am too dizzy from its contents to
   contain my barren thoughts,
So here they are.

My palm tree stands here in its pot,
Dracaena marginata, so the label reads.
Its fallen leaves remind me that it needs my love,
Some water from the tap.

I have a crate that from the wreck did fall,
   And from it comes the ocean's call.
Soap-suds and oily films do crest its waves of smutty laughter.
On Sunday nights one fish my line does catch.
Here is the news.

The spring that keeps me sane,
Pours endless words before my sight.
They tell me you are there, so heed my plight.
No poem this, tonight.

So I must rest upon this rock,
An empty place where I alone
   Can count the grains of sand,
And the monotone tick of an alarmless clock
Wakes another day.

If this has washed up on your shore,
Somewhere in this bleak archipelago,
Then chain it on, five pence a copy, maybe ten.
If comes at last to heart of gold, just knock on any door.
Reach out the hand of God.

***Peter J Bolton***

## MESSAGE IN A BOTTLE

You're trapped on a tiny island,
With no mod cons to hand.
But with paper and pencil you think you're really grand.
Not many folk think to carry an aid to point out which
Direction they could be, and fewer still use arts that could
Be used with dignity.

I'd try to describe where I was and give a rough outline of
What had happened to me,
Then I'd try to find shelter and wait very faithfully.
Don't add too many orders from an irrational mind,
Just ask that your saviour be simple, true and kind.

***Betty Green***

## Waiting For You

I'm lost, stuck forever
For all eternity.
Please bring me hope
And everyday I'll pray
That you will be here
To end this misery.
You are the bringer of freedom
And when you come,
The sun will fade
The sea will hush.
I will be waiting
Waiting for you.

***Lucy Webb***

## Message In A Bottle

The words that I had longed to hear
Never had been said
Now the time had come and gone
For my love was dead

Who'd never said he loved me
But strange words that he said
The last time he'd spoken
Rang hollow in my head.

There was a silent sailing ship
On swirling silent sea
Contained within a bottle
By a note he'd left for me.

'Do not keep the model
Drop it on the ground.'
I did as I was bidden
It broke without a sound

As from within this treasure
There came a golden flow
Of waves that held a message
'I love you more than you could know.'

***Anita Richards***

## LOYALTY

*(Dedicated to, Elsa & Nat Perez, Ana De Freitas & Philip Vile, Dorit Zack & Takis Kalogroulis)*

To my dearest friends
Who make my life abundant
Knowing how much they care
And I mean to them . . .

You are the fertile fields!
That I once cultivated
Sharing dreams and trust
Out of friendship and love

Now . . .
With overwhelming generosity,
. . . Of your loving hearts
I'm harvesting fruits offered
With my immense gratitude

'Friends' . . . Divine word,
Of harmony and brotherhood
'Love' . . . Breaks all boundaries
Giving me freedom and hope

Your beautiful thoughts
Are messenger doves
Bringing to my table . . .
Food in starving days
And handing the glass to quench
. . . My insatiable thirst

Your memories of my past
Fulfil this present of mine
Receiving them with joyful tears
They light up my road so dark

A road . . .
That I must travel alone
But with your words . . .

And caring thoughts
In this maze I don't feel lost
And if it weren't for them
. . . I could not carry on

As a man of many lands
I ride on the sullen winds
Seeking for new tomorrows
Away from my last yesterdays

Your letters are for me; Wings
Healers of turmoil and seclusion
You are few and very special
Like a legion by my side

With your presence in my life
I have need for nothing else
Thanking my Father for the gift
Of your loyalty beyond doubt.

***Eduardo Del-Rio Escalona***

## A Message In A Bottle

Strolling in the morning sun
Waves lapping around my feet
Cooled by the ocean spray
A haven from the soaring heat.

The clear blue carpet
Shimmering in its majesty
Provides a vast horizon
And a glint of hope.

But as the days go by
No ships have neared
My castaway island
A masqueraded paradise.

By day, a lonely hermit
With barely any food to eat
By night, a frightened animal
Without a shelter to retreat.

But as my message drifts
With the ever turning tide
Under the moonlit stars, I dream
Deliverance is nigh.

***Patricia Anne Turner***

## MESSAGE IN A BOTTLE

To the finder of this bottle don't discard if as a joke,
What's written here may really be my last and final hope.
When I set sail from Dartmouth, the town that is my home
I always thought the seven seas were there for me to roam.
Bayard's cove slipped quietly by, a favourite place of mine,
I looked at it not knowing it could be the final time.
My boat was strong, and proud she sailed as we headed for the sea,
She was called the 'Robert Hardy' - I named her after me.
From North to South Atlantic we sailed determinedly
Until a mighty wave destroyed my boat, and almost me.
And now a desert island is my sparse and dismal host
Washed up where I'm not quite sure off the Tanzanian coast.
I have hunger, thirst and scorching heat and ocean all around.
All my instincts tell me this could be my final ground
But whilst I'm still quite sound in mind, my greetings to all send
And tell those that have loved me that I loved them to the end.
I know the year's 2000 - it's about the 4th of May
And if you read this message try and find me right away!

***John Mason***

## Leave My Mark

Footprints upon footprints
Each one my own
I've left my mark here alright
The sole static tree has no bark
I've carved my initials so often
The tree could be on a diet plan
It's stark naked and vulnerable
Like a rock star's fan
I worshipped you sun
You repaid me by burning and wearing me out
The ship I frequently see
Is a mirage, there's just blue sea and me
Poor tree, I didn't mean to harm thee
There was nothing else to do
Memories of wanting to be alone when in a crowd
Constantly haunt me
Each passing lifeless breeze
Reminds me how lonely I am
I wish for a boat full of life
Living alone just doesn't feel right.

***John Beals***

## HEARTS APART

Remember
For ever
I love you.
Never again
Are apart,
Staying
With me
For a life time,
The distance
Between us
So far,
Pulling us
Closer together,
The strength
We have in our
Hearts,
Undying was love
From the start,
Away from each other
We can't,
Existing I know
You are lonely,
For me
The feeling's the same,
Thinking of you, forever
I hold again and again,
Writing this message
Of love,
This island
My life it has changed.

***Martin Toyne***

## SEE THAT GIRL

You see that girl standing at the bar
She might be drunk but she knows who you are
She wants you for a little chat
Are you really staying there still sat.

You see that girl standing at the bar
She might be drunk but she has a car
She says that she can give a ride
Are you still stood here alone outside.

You see that girl standing at the bar
She might be drunk but she is still going far
For she is still inside your mind
Upon the beach and in the sea so kind.

***Keith L Powell***

## My Lifeline

The storm grew worse each passing hour,
The lightning struck, we lost our power;
The waves grew large and rocked our ship,
For those on board 'twas hard to grip.

In early hours of the night,
We found ourselves without a light;
'Twas then that final damage done,
Our ship was lost, the storm had won.

With lifebelt firmly, set in place,
I slowly fought to win my race;
To save my life and reach some isle,
It really proved the longest mile.

The shore was reached with mammoth fight,
I lay exhausted through the night;
At break of dawn I glimpsed my isle,
Some sand, some palms, a stream, a smile.

As strength returned, I made my way,
To focal point along the Bay;
I hoisted shirt upon a branch,
Some ship might spot me with a glance.

In empty bottle I wrote my note,
I told all world of Isle remote;
My hopes, my prayers, my dreams wrote down,
Just wrapped in bottle that would not drown.

I threw my lifeline out to sea,
With hopes and prayers to make me free;
Would someone, somewhere, read my note,
Then rescue me, from Isle remote?

***John Paulley***

## My Kids

With your cornflower eyes
Hay coloured hair
Spindly leg
Missing teeth
With Barbie on your mind
Imagination running wild
My kids.

I wish I could see you afresh
Not through tired eyes
See the way your faces glow
When I say
Let's play a game
See the anticipation from your view
Of some paper and some glue
A room that's dying to be messed up
My kids.

My sweet, loud, beautiful, noisy, slightly messy,
Harmless, innocent kids
My kids.
I love you.
Mum.

***Alison M Craxford***

## TRADE WINDS

A tiny island
Cover'd in sand
Is where, I chance to land
A tiny cave, away from the heat
Soft warm waves
Ripple round my feet.
Is where I'm going to stay.
I've found some berries
Sadly no sherry.
If a boat - yacht, you have
Or a canoe, will do
To take me off, this lost horizon.
We could sail off,
Into the 'wide blue yonder'
So hurry - don't ponder
Just follow the waves
To the cave
With champagne and oysters
Who wants a cave?
So sweet aloha
Make waves soon.

***Margaret Parnell***

## Horizon Beyond

Although we've never met
Though I speak to you most days
The image of you in my thoughts is
You're over six feet tall and interesting
I know you have a boat - cause you're a
Fisherman - I've been told - so before you rescue
Me, can we use the sailcloth - shelter from the sun
We could walk in the warm shallows
Leaving damp footprints in the sand
We could talk for hours - you could even
Teach me to fish - little success - to date
And leave before the sun sets in the west
Must go it's high tide and I've a
Turtle to feed.
(New friend - little conversation).

***David Charles***

## SOS

A shipwreck caused my arrival here,
far from home and all those I hold dear.
Such a beautiful place to be,
lots of sand beside the sea.
I tried to fish, oh what a mess -
the line I made out of my dress!

The sun, so hot, beats down all day,
clouds very rarely stray this way.
To find a drink is not so hard,
but food - I'm not just hungry, I'm starved!
To catch a lizard isn't easy -
like snakes, they make my tummy queasy!

Spiders really aren't my scene,
and scorpions - well I just scream!
Not being a monkey, I struggle to climb trees,
besides the fruit is theirs if you please!
So I scratch around to find what I may -
what I'd give for a steak today!

I shiver all night and sweat all day,
my attempt at a shelter fell away!
Really I need a D.I.Y man,
so, please God, shipwreck one for me, if you can!
He'd keep me warm at night and protect me day by day -
please, oh please, send one this way!

But if a human hand finds my bottle note,
please take me from here in your boat!
Desert Island Discs they can keep,
I'd swap for a feather bed in which to sleep!
It's beautiful here I'll grant You that God -
but I'm obviously a 'home comfort' bod!

***Margi Hughes***

## My Message To You

I have always wanted to go on a cruise
But you didn't want me to go.
You didn't want to come along with me.
You didn't want to know.

Life on the liner was divine
Floating along the sea like a leaf,
Until that awful noise, and terrible crash,
When the liner hit a reef.

Propelled by the sea, holding on to a plank,
I drifted to this tiny place.
Exhausted, and tired, I laid on the sand,
The hot sun burning my face.

With no food to eat, and no water to drink
I crawled around looking for shade
To hide, and to rest, from the soaring heat,
And trying not to be afraid.

My hairs all in knots, my clothes torn and ripped,
No mirror to see how I look.
I long for the day I'll be back on the land.
How I wish that I had a good book!

I don't know the time, I sleep when I'm tired,
My dreams are of you, and friends at home.
When I lie awake, and look at this place,
I wonder, 'Why did I roam?'

My lips are cracked and my tongue is sore,
I drink what tiny drop of dew I can find.
What I'd give for a meal, and a real cup of tea.
The thought of food is really unkind.

If you receive this message, please think of me
Lost on this barren island.
I wish I had listened to all that you said
To be home again, would be grand.

Until we meet again, if ever we do
My love to you I send.
Remember the good days, and the good times we had.
My love for you, will live on, until the end.

***Joan Smith***

## Message In A Bottle

Should one day this bottle is found
        by someone sane on hallowed ground,
in God's name please hear my plea
        and save me from insanity,
one thousand leagues sou, sou, west
        believe my Sir, I do not jest,
three months, one week and two whole days
        this time I've had to mend my ways,
what food there was, has long gone
        just nuts, berries and prayer and song,
if someone then should sail this way
        not I think, within my days,
and if by chance my body is found
        please take me home to hallowed ground
there lay me down to rest in peace
        then only, will my wandering cease.

***D Richards***

## JUST A QUICK NOTE

With pen in hand I've tried to write this note to you.
I know where I stand, but what am I to do?
I've found so many things to say since we're so far apart,
How can I write on paper what I feel in my heart?
Those simple things you gave are worth the world to me,
And each of them I claim; you can't take my memories.
So many things were left unsaid; I don't know where to start.
How can I write on paper what I feel in my heart?
How can I write on paper what I'm feeling deep inside?
Words to you would last no longer than it takes the ink to dry
A love as sweet as yours and mine deserves another start
How can I write what I feel in my heart?

***Sam Clarke***

## Forget Me Not

Forget me not when the sun goes down
And the moon sets in the opaque sky,

Forget me not when you lay me down
To rest for a little while,

Forget me not when the fire that burns
Turns to sombre ashen spill,

Forget me not when I am gone
For the spirit never dies,
It carries on eternally
In our children's eyes,

Forget me not so I shall remember
That our souls are entwined,
Together,
Forever.

***Sally Bush***

## PHONEY

Help someone, I'm desperate,
Please answer, please do,
I'm here all alone,
Washed up and so blue,
If you do find this bottle
And you read what I say,
Believe me, it's urgent,
No time for delay,
Don't call out the army,
Don't call out the police,
Don't contact my mother,
My nephew or niece,
Don't call out the coastguard,
Nor the navy deploy -
Just give me a ring
On my mobile, old boy!

***Peter Davies***

## PARADISE

Tropical island going cheap . . .
Lacks a house, nowhere to sleep -
The shellfish have screwed up my guts,
Palm trees haven't any nuts . . .
No pretty bugs - the things all bite,
The constant sun is far too bright.
Bird songs all made up of shrieks,
Untameable, just see those beaks!
Paradise is lost for me;
Come to that . . . you can have it *free*.

***Di Bagshawe***

## ABANDONED

I'm stressed, depressed
And my tears flow
Like an avalanche
From my eyes.
The lies of my friends echo
In my head, for they said
They'd come back for me.
Their broken promises
Like grains of sand falling through my hand
Are their tokens of their care!
I am left, so bereft
With no sign on the horizon line,
And I wait, and faint
Only grazing on the maze
Of thoughts in my mind.
Unkind!
This bare place provides nothing,
And hides me from view,
Burying me as treasure.
But I have no more pleasure
In my dreams and schemes
To quit this scene of mean company.
All have failed.
Here I am nailed.
Please! Throw me a rope of hope
That I may cling to, and sing,
And be freed from the greed
Of this island
And no more abandoned.

***Judith Thomas***

## A Saving Plea

I am sending this message
With hope in my heart
That someone somewhere will find it
For here I am stranded on this isle
I know not where, roasting from the heat

I was sailing from South Africa
Heading for Australia
When hit by a freak storm
And here I am alone and forlorn
Feeling jolly warm

My plight is desperate
Drinking water is low
Have found a small stream
Yet it needs the rain to grow

Please find me soon
There is so much I want to live for
You think a lot all alone under the moon
And there is someone special that I adore
And I need to get home to tell him so

I need my daughters
To see their faces once more
I need to tell them I love them so
Something that normally I forego
Help me please find me soon
So home I can go, to all that I adore.

***Janet Fish***

## MISSING

Strolling along the shoreline
as we did so often before,
familiar waves swirling, rippling,
returning again to shore.

Grasses dance and sing in the dunes
to the salt breeze's tune, just the same.
This time I stop . . . listen too long
I can hear them whisper your name.

The easiest thing now, with all purpose gone,
on this tide, just slip away.
No one now to care too much,
nothing so dear to make me stay.

Another tide ebbs, revealing the rocks,
seaweed slumbers again, as water leaves land.
Perpetual movements of this vast earth
and our precious lives, just grains of sand.

***T P Bradley***

## PARADISE?

O harken to my plea
Make haste and rescue me.
The sun it burns so fierce
Hot needles my skin pierce.
No shade or shelter here
To help placate my fear.
A deep trench in the sand
I've dug with my weak hand.
A quick dip in the sea
Will help to freshen me.
I pray for cloud and rain
To ease my searing pain.
I cannot build a raft
Or any other craft,
No trees or tools to hand
I'm really at a stand
Is that a fin I see
To make a meal of me?
What joy, a periscope
Has come to give me hope.
Just in the nick of time
For me to end this rhyme.

***Jennifer Stella Smeed***

## MESSAGE IN A BOTTLE

Tell Mary
I miss her . . .

Freckled face
Fair features
Fulsome embrace
Familiar peaches

Tell Mary
I remember her . . .

Foolish fears
Faint heart
False ears
The *feisty tart*

Tell Mary
I love her . . .

*Where she is!*

*Do not rescue.*

***R J Westwell***

## MESSAGE IN A BOTTLE

*(Psalm 119: Verse 1706 -*
*Deliver me according to thy Word)*

I've been a castaway about a year
I've done what I can with what I found here
I learnt quite a bit from a Mission friend
On survival without money to spend
From these date palms I shake fruit to the ground
I drink fresh water from pools which I found
These dates from the palms give me energy
But oh I'd just love a big mug of tea!
I rescued some rope from pieces of plank
It could well be from some wessel that sank
Unravelling rope I made a fish line
And to a stout branch I fastened this twine.
I found some wire to make a fish hook
Then dug up some worms but shivered and shook . . .
I hate squirmy things but I'm really stuck
I must catch some fish or die on this spot!
The sun and some glass with pieces of bark
helped light a fire for 'supper' at dark.
It's nice for a while, this ocean so blue
But I just thank God for this bottle too
I've a pen to write this message to you
I've given some clues to rescue me too!
So how did I get here? To all of this?
That's a trade secret, I tell for a kiss!

Come to my rescue from this tiny isle
Please bring me some sweets and warmth of your smile!

PS - 'I love you' - I hope you love me?
I'll heat up some water, you bring some tea!

***Lisa Gore***

## Wish You Were Here

This is just to say
From me, a castaway,
I don't want rescuing before 2002,
There's so much here I have to do,
There's a shelter, marked Desert Island Discs,
Don't worry, I'm not taking any risks!
It's not a problem finding food to eat,
Fish, strange berries and nuts for a treat.
There may be mice or a plump brown rat
But I'd have to be desperate to chance cooking that!
The flowers are heavenly, the whole island is scented.
Long, lazy, calm days make me contented.
I think I've discovered a dodo's remains
Were they dumb creatures without any brains?
Just think, modern science could bring it to life,
You'd have someone famous to boast for your wife.
Can you tell Alice it's wonderland here,
Mythical creatures, strange and wild to revere.
Doctor Dolittle would like to come too,
Parrots, maybe dragons or a push-me-pull-you?
How come I've arrived in the Indian Ocean?
Promise you won't tell Steve of my devotion?
His five Olympic medals inspired *me* to row,
I just got a *bit* lost when I left Borneo!
I know my family will think 'Grandma's gone mad'!
But travel, exercise and effort can't be all bad!
Of course *we'll* be home for aunty's 100th birthday,
*If* I can persuade *her* it's best not to stay!

***Susan Holmquist***

## I Still Miss Someone

I send this message for you today
I hope you will find it I pray
I shall always love you although we are apart
Your love and guidance are here in my heart
No one can take my memories away
Although you are far away
No distance or time can ever erase
Those lovely blue eyes and smiley face
So I hope you receive this message
That I send with all my love
Now presiding with God above.

Love you forever.

***Glenis Dando***

## MAROONED

I've missed the boat, I am marooned,
On an island far from shore
I thought it would be paradise
But it isn't anymore.

There's crabs galore and fishes
But I cannot catch the things.
The seagulls cry and fly away
On their graceful outstretched wings.

But alas I have no wings to fly
No raft, no ship in sight
Just a message in a bottle
To tell you of my plight.

So will you come and rescue me
Whoever you may be?
I'll be your friend forever
I'm tired of sand and sea,
And how I long for someone
To share a pot of tea.

***Isobel Laffin***

## RESCUE ME

I have spent so much of my time
Just standing on this empty beach.
The crowded world I left behind
Seems forever out of reach.

I think about my beautiful wife
And my daughters every single day,
And the thought of how much I miss them
Obscured my island with clouds of grey.

I often pray that a ship would pass
And pluck me from this shore.
I'd love to see the look on my family's face
When I step inside the door.

So, if you are the fortunate one
Who plucked my bottle from the sea;
I pray that you'll do the right thing,
And come and rescue me.

Please come and rescue me,
And finally put an end to my pain.
Please be my undying salvation
And let me see my loved ones again.

Please come and rescue me
Because I'm lonely and hungry for love.
And I don't know how much longer
I can keep praying to the Lord above.

I know the Lord can hear me
And if he could, he would give me wings.
In him I'll continue to put my faith
And wait and see what tomorrow brings.

***Peter Steele***

## MESSAGE IN A BOTTLE

Mamma abandoned me
On this remote Island
To me, an unknown destiny.
Said she'd return, that was three days ago
No inhabitants, I'm alone
Without food or water.
Just enough strength to write this message.
Put it in a bottle, watch it glide
On the crest of the waves.

I have faith, I pray
That's how I spend the day.
Nights are cold, I shelter beside the rocks
Suck the lichen for moisture.
Perhaps a fisherman will find my message,
I know Mamma won't return
Tracks of her truck are still visible
On the damp sand
She sped away at great speed
Without a goodbye.
I'm eight years old and so alone
I trust God will direct my destiny
Pray someone will rescue me soon,
Very soon.

Abandoned child.

***Frances Gibson***

## ULTIMATUM

People pitied me or scorned my plight
upon the craft to distant land;
my love, I abandoned ship one night
in deep despair, you understand?
Colour is sharp and my rations small,
bearded I stay on isle retreat
alone, disquieted, yet I recall
timed with you eternally sweet.
This note I write to a world of dream.
Where would you be and do you care?
Your refusal hurt and yet I seem
to feel your presence everywhere.
If our lovely days are now as nought
relinquish me to scarlet birds,
ignore these lines in this bottle caught,
broken inarticulate words,
leave me to the flame fired juices,
sun-baked unsympathetic earth,
skies of strident greens and puces
if that is what I'm merely worth.
Fates hold this missive in their power;
should you have second thoughts, repent
relieve me from this stolen hour
where surely once magicians went
forming gaudy ruthless bloom,
gargantuan empurpled bough;
save me or leave me to my doom
spurn me or with new love endow.

***Ruth Deviat***

## Bottled Loneliness

I'm all alone and very sad,
Sitting here on my dung heap,
I have a bottle here to fill,
I'll send it home with loads of love,
(Can love sink parcels,
mine's so full -
    and heavy too?)

I'm thinking of your lovely cakes
And wishing they were here,
I get so tired of fishy things,
I get fed up with smelly clothes,
The loneliness just gets me down,
I should be glad of anyone,
    even my *crossest* teacher.

I'd be so grateful for a friend,
Someone who'd answer back,
They could have money from my bank,
I'll never more be greedy.
But what I really, really want
Is my dearest, loving mum,
If only *she* were with me here,
I'd make her lots of promises,
    and I'd keep them, yes, I'd *keep* them all.

My mum would hardly know me now,
I am so quiet and gentle,
But I'm just the same inside
And oh, I long to see her.
    Oh Mum! Dear Mum, please fetch me home.
    I'm crying out to see you.

***Frida Harris***

## ISLE OF PEACE

On this desert island,
With only my faith,
I wash my hands of a greedy world,
Happy to be alone.

Surrounded by treasures made of the Lord,
No finer possessions
Could I ever afford.

Pain and strife left far behind,
Only the good times,
Visit my mind.

Forget my name
Just leave me here
With only my faith
I have no fear.

***Jane Rennie***

## FUGITIVE FROM JUNK FOOD

This paradise island's all very well,
But sometimes it really feels like hell.
Oh, I know, I shouldn't moan,
But it's boring here all on your own,
No one to talk to, nothing to do,
But sit around and think of food:
Bucket of chicken, Kentucky Fried,
Onion rings, coleslaw on the side.
Big Mac, large fries, a milkshake or two,
Tikka masala, Bombay aloo,
Egg and chips with a fried slice,
Thai green curry, fragrant rice,
Bacon sandwich, toast and cheese,
Haddock with scraps and mushy peas,
What I wouldn't give for one of these.

A strange thing happened yesterday
As I was going on my way
To sunbathe near my favourite tree
And dabble my toes into the sea,
I found a bottle, very old,
And when I had scraped off the mould
I had an idea to get in touch
With the people I miss so much.
I thought for a moment, then began:
'One Hawaiian, large, deep-pan
Extra mushrooms, double ham,
Add some sweetcorn if you can,
And don't forget jalapeños.'
Depending on the tidal flows,
My note might float to Domino's.

*Nicky Adams*

## A Rescue

Please pick up this bottle someone, there's a message there to find,
If God will grant my rescue I'll leave wickedness behind.
Loving parents, sweetheart, my love I send to you,
I'm desperate, starving, frightened and don't know what to do.
Forgive that day I kicked the dog and hid my brother's bike,
Told a lie to save a clout when Gran called me a little tyke.
It was me who stole the girlfriend from my brother's mate,
We had a fight, he was right, now he's full of hate.
I look at the horizon, can only see the sea,
Longing for a pint of beer and wonder what you have for tea.
Mum, you made the best roast beef, I dribble at the thought,
Remember when my shirt was ripped? Not on a nail, I fought.
My thoughts are incoherent, exhaustion takes its toll,
Be brave I say, to myself, please God save my soul.
I promise I will mend my ways if someone rescues me,
Come and get me quickly, or I am lost at sea.

***P Evans***

## Coming On Home To You

It's been a long and winding road babe
And my path has not been straight
But I'm coming on home to you
Meet me as I come on home to you.

Been down the road of sorrow more than I care to remember
Taken all the wrong turnings in life
But I'm coming on home to you
Coming on home to you
See me as I walk the road to you.
And in the winter
When there's no one else around
Not knowing where I'm bound
And no one makes a sound
I'll be coming on home to you babe
Coming on home to you.

Life sometimes goes and gets me down babe
For I'm a lonely sort of guy
But when I see you babe
I'm really coming on home to you
Coming to meet me at the station gate.

Don't go and close the door on me babe
Don't kick me in the teeth
I want to come on home to you babe
Coming on home to you
As soon as the day is through.
And in the summer
When the sun shines on me
We will be free
I will make you see
I'll be coming on home to you
Coming on home to you.

***Philip Loudon***

## STAMINA

Starting the morning with God
in prayer
or in communicating with nature
or with one another in love
is good
helping bring the creator
to all our daze.

***Robert D Shooter***

## A Long Swim Home

If you are reading this message
Can you do something for me
Give hugs and kisses to my family
And bring me a cup of tea

I found my way here by accident
The moon was showing the way
I wait so long to be rescued
The night becoming confused with the day

I miss my friends and family
And going to work on the train
The sun is so very hot here
I'm even missing the rain

I'm starting to talk to myself now
And answering back, it's sad
Oh please can somebody find me
I feel I am going mad

I would like to say I'm sorry
To everyone I've made cry
I feel that my life is over
If only a ship would come by

On this island that's now my prison
I lay down to sleep or die
I dream of my family at home
And restless in sleep, I cry

The dawn breaks, the sun rises
I feel so weak and so thin
I might see my loved ones again
I decided I'm going to swim.

***Angela Eames***

## SALTWATER SURVIVOR

Castaway on this island, I'll just have to do my best
Looks like I'm the only survivor - lucky - yes, I guess
Eating just berries and coconuts, drinking spring water oh so clear
No hamburgers - no pies and chips - there's no fast food round here.

I'm sick of seeing yellow, the blazing sun and all that sand
Can somebody grant me just one wish with a magic wand
How long have I been here, it seems like many years
Oh boy what would I give for a beef sandwich and an ice cold beer.

I've no music to listen to, no more nagging from the wife
In fact I don't have anything in my sad and lonely life
Being stuck here on this island, watching tides ebb and flow
I'm walking round in circles cos there's no where else to go.

I'm getting extremely bored now - I might do something daft
At the moment if a boat came ashore, I'd smash it up and build a raft
I've lost so much weight, no one back home would recognise me
I hope I soon get rescued from this haven in the sea.

I ain't spotted no boats or ships out on the horizon
No planes in the sky, passing the burning sun
I've thrown six messages in bottles into the frothy sea
They all give my location - lost at sea - please rescue me.

***Leigh Smart***

## WHERE ARE YOU?

I've got an empty bottle
So a refill I could use
But inside I send this message
Which I hope you will peruse.
It's not that I'm alone just now
Upon this desert isle
But food and drink are really short
Both going out of style.
If I'm very lucky
And the map you understand
Perhaps you'll come and rescue me
From all this sun and sand.
I used to spend a bob or two
To visit shores like this
But all that English weather
Alas, I've come to miss.
'Shades of Treasure island'
Though there's nothing buried here
X marks the spot for me my friend.
I'd better make that clear!
Time's running out, I fancy
My hopes begin to wain
This last communication
I shall not write again.
So if you'd like to see me
And I really hope you do
This 'message in a bottle'
I have written just for you!

***T G Bloodworth***

## MESSAGE IN A BOTTLE

I scrambled from the cold, wet sea
And thought I'd reached eternity.
At last a place to rest my head,
Weary limbs that felt like lead.
At least now I can feel warm
Away from sharks that do such harm.
I crawled across the sandy beach
To try the little shade to reach,
But it seemed so far away
I was sure I'd die that day.
All alone on this island bare,
No strength to move - who's going to care?
My stomach thinks my throat's been cut
By the noise it's making in my gut.
My lips are cracked and oh so sore
There's no fresh water on this shore.
I found this bottle beneath the sand
Whilst blindly scrabbling with my hand.
My faithful pen is all that's left,
I clung to it though I felt bereft;
And this paper here I found nearby
I'm so relieved I want to cry.
But I must save energy
To send this note with heartfelt plea.
So should you open this bottle - please
Bring me water, bread and cheese.
For everything else I'll gladly wait
But hurry, hurry before it's too late -
Because I'm too young to be knocking on Heaven's gate.

***Joan Earle Broad***

## A MESSAGE IN A BOTTLE

Save me! I'm out of luck.
I'm badly stuck
In mid-ocean

Help! I'm all alone.
On a block of stone
Robbed of motion.

Please intercede!
Sitting on seaweed
Cools the bottom

There's rawness around my epiglottis,
A tickly throat serving notice.
And, I shiver

From my nose fluids drip,
Running down my upper lip,
Like a river.

Inside my skull my brain squeezes,
Pressure escapes in surging sneezes.
Influenza!

Retrace this bottle
By the trail of snottle,
Make me glad.

Carry me home
Away from foam
To a warm bed.

Hear my plea
Can't you see
I'm nearly dead.

***James Taylor***

## LONG VACATION

The waves pounded at the boat, next thing
I was on dry land
The whole of my body covered
In sand . . .?

I stood up shocked, just miles of sea . . .?
On a shipwrecked island, staring right at me

Maybe it's nice when you go on holiday
But this is a joke . . .?
Is there anyone else here, or, is there just
Me, this bloke . . .?

Weeks went by, and months, I made
Me a little hut
Three meals a day of fish, fish, coconuts
And more coconuts.

My wife must be wondering where the
Hell I have gone
Never thought I'd be Robinson Crusoe
Now my beard, is two foot long . . .?

An old bottle washed on the shore, and yes . . . some
Paper in it . . .
It's a long way to find a pen, so I wrote
In fish blood, that ought to do
The trick . . .?

I threw the bottle into the sea . . .?
Inside the words would someone please
Bloody help me . . .?

I sit on the rocks, wishing I was
Back home
No beer, no cigars, just all alone . . .?

I wish I could tell the wife I'll be
Home tomorrow
A plane went past yesterday, but missed me
Oh no . . .

***D Riches***

## Desert Island Experience

Here I am, marooned, alone.
Restrictions, deprivations, struggles, fear;
Solution so unknown . . .
But your spirit is here.

Now I'm thankful to be warm,
Cast on this relatively sheltered sphere,
Not perished in the storm -
And your spirit's here.

Talking to you brings me light.
Your caring thoughts are comfortingly near
Through darkest stormy night,
For your spirit is here.

Cast out on the waves, I send
This message: 'Rescue me' - or, as 'twas penned
Long past by John, your friend,
'Come, Lord Jesus, Amen.'

***Elma Heath***

## FROM THIS ISLAND

My spirit soars upon the wind
My heart in sun shines bright
My words to you I send in waves
Of love and hope and light.

For we are all like grains of sand
Upon some golden shore
Who sparkle as we share our lives
And love each other more.

My gift to you, the gift of peace
I send with open heart
Have courage, faith in all you do
Take action from the start.

Think carefully, constructively,
For you have much to give
Be positive in all you do
You have one life to live.

And should my message reach you from
This island in the sea,
I trust that you will find a way
To come and visit me.

***Katrina Shepherd***

## IN THE DRINK

As a millionaire and cruising, aboard a super liner
In sartorial perfection, my clothes were pure designer
The cuisine was par excellence, with champagne by the case
Life was simply heavenly, not a problem did I face

But one night I drank unwisely, and went o'er the starboard side
And was promptly swept away, by a racing, foaming tide
Then the wind blew up my shirt, and exposed the silken tail
And luckily for me, it functioned like a sail

No longer was life heavenly, it was more akin to hell
I lost all count of time, as I hurtled through the swell
My scheduled port of call, should have been a week in Thailand
Instead of which I landed on a tiny desert island

Of shelter there was none, just sand and sea and sun
Not another soul in sight, I was the only one
Apart from some marauding sharks, a fearsome looking bunch
Who clearly were considering a rather special lunch

For many days I just survived, eating seaweed from the sands
Plus water from the skies, caught in closely coupled hands
My only two possessions were a little pencil stub
And a card confirming membership, of a most exclusive club

All this while I felt that time was getting shorter
Then I found a bottle, as used for mineral water
With pencil stub and card, I wrote a last despairing plea
Put it in the bottle, and cast it to the sea

My cry for help was found, I was rescued just in time
This then is the moral, within this little rhyme
Champagne can bring disaster, indeed one may well die
But stick to aqua puro, and you'll probably get by!

***J Power***

## Message In A Bottle

Here is my message in a bottle
That tour guide I could easily throttle
She said the cruise will be like fun
Lay on deck in the afternoon sun
Then came that great big wave
This bottle and paper is all I did save.
There's a cave in which we sleep
And feed on a flock of sheep.
We have to boil up the sea water
That is the captain, me and his virgin daughter.
The captain has a very strange laugh
And watches me when I take a bath.
Do you think I am losing grip
When I wash I will not strip.
We made a beacon on the hill
The girl told me she is on the pill.
Yesterday we saw a passing plane
How I wish we had gone to Spain.
We have been here for one whole week
I'm eating the captain as we speak.

***Colin Allsop***

## I'll Bounce Back Again

*(After 'Still I Rise' by Maya Angelou)*

You may shatter my resistance
with a barrage of abuse
upon the battlefields of life
for which there's no excuse
and you may crucify my feelings
on some bleeding cross of pain
beneath a god-forsaken sky
but I'll bounce back again.

You may conquer my resources
in the fortress of my soul
before my senses can redress
the balance of control
and you may clip my wings of freedom
in an effort to restrain
my flight into eternity
but I'll bounce back again.

You may crush me like a flower
in the garden of my mind
where only seeds of love's neglect
prove difficult to find
and you may revel in my downfall
when despair has left its stain
upon the threshold of belief
but I'll bounce back again.

***Iaian W Wade***

## THE FREEDOM OF TRUTH

As I sit burnt in the scorching heat,
Parched with the lessening of life,
I wonder who might find my message,
A lost soul in some distant future,

My life is not yet complete,
Yet flashing by me to the fore,
Of good times then memories no longer to come,
My priorities have somewhat changed,

Gone are the thoughts of house, car or belongings,
Replaced by what I should or should not have done,
Comforted by the actions of adding to,
Have made me see the person I have now become,

My yearning just to say goodbye with a loving touch,
Of family whom I have loved so much,
No price can buy a precious last embrace,
The face I wear is now my final grace,

As I wonder what I have learnt along the way,
And look around no person do I see,
I do not know the who, the when, or why,
I only know my God inside will surely set me free . . . !

***Martin Crawley***

## MESSAGE IN A BOTTLE

It's been so long
Since I've been home
I've spent three years
Living on my own

I've had no letters
I've seen no friends
How long before
This nightmare ends?

It started out
Our dream come true
Now I've lost all
Including you

I never meant
To let you go
I held your hand
I loved you so

The waves turned out
To be too strong
They pulled us down
And now you're gone

Every day I watch for you
Out against the waves so blue
Now and then the hope drifts in
But floats out with the tide again

Maybe one day you will find
This message that I'll leave behind
With tears of life remember me,
'Cause I'll remember you

And the day that fate took over us
On that sea so blue

***Kelly Souten***

## I Would Look For Something In A Bottle

Ah ha
A bottle
Just what I was looking for
My lips parched
Of the sweet rum
To drown my throat
Yet to someone who may come to this island
Let me free
From my pains
All that I play to be free of this moment
Rum
It seems
Does wonders
To bring hope of a ship
This bottle drunk
Some more
Collected and hoarded
To drink it down
Thought comes of someone a long time ago
If that is what I would drink to or becomes me in other ways
Take my misery away for the moment
This I ask you oh bottle
You may as I would wish bring hope for my future.

***C J Bayless***

## Bottled

I'm only a note that someone wrote
And placed in a bottle at sea.
Thrown as a joke, those laughing folk
Had no care what happened to me -

I just turned and tossed, somehow I'm lost,
In the ocean so wild and free,
But I mustn't mope, I'll just have to cope,
With a situation beyond me!

Oh! Somewhere I'm found! But I'll be bound
To wonder my fate you see -
But such is my joy, being found by a boy,
Who treasures this keepsake - that's me - I'm free!

***Ivy Cawood***

## The Pirates' Cook

It might have been old Blackbeard perhaps that Captain Hook
I don't quite know who did it, I didn't get to look
I was working in the galley as assistant pirate cook
Making up the captain's lunch by the ancient pirate's book

I don't know how I did it, I put the salt in twice
To hide the salty flavour, I added extra spice
The dish was served to the captains, they said it wasn't nice
That I'd been very careless and would have to pay the price

The sea was clear and greeny as I walked the pirate's plank
Beyond the far horizon my former shipmates sank
I made it to an island (there's a dolphin I must thank)
The place is far from paradise on that I must be frank

So if you get this bottle and read my little note
I'd like to see some rescue men come in a rescue boat
And could they please bring with them some baccy for a smoke
A jug of thick black pirate's rum to ease my long-parched throat

***Ray Ryan***

## ES-OH-ES

Help - island - name unknown

How did I come to be on this isle
The surrounding sea stretching mile upon mile
Did I land, swim or fall from the sky?
Although that is now somewhat by-the-by.

Is there a simple way off I begin to wonder
This sunny isle - or is it one of rain and thunder
If it is a pleasant peaceful one
Perhaps I'll stay here longer just for fun.

What did I do wrong to experience this
At home, did I leave a dirty dish?
If this is such, I do apologise
And a route back home I'll have to devise.

Until I can sail off on the ever blue water
Food and drink must truly be sought after
Build a good fire as oven - and signal flare
Being alone my harvesting I'll not have to share.

Do I like my own company, this I'll find out
No one to tell me that loudly I shout
I'll be able to sing all out of tune
From a rostrum of a natural dune.

Perhaps life here will not be so bad after all
But how did I come - by land, sea or sky-fall?
Maybe I'll wake up with soft pillow under my head
And all this has been a night-time dream instead.

Please help me, my message pleads as penned
For a stamped addressed envelope I cannot send
But this bottle on the beach I have found
So please help me, dear folk, where my plea comes aground.

***Barbara Allix***

## MESSAGE IN A BOTTLE

As it
happens
I have only a few
words left. My pencil is short.
Sharpening it on a pebble - as I had to,
I have worn it right down to a one-inch bit.
So it's very difficult to write much with it
on this damp beer mat which I'll try
and squeeze into this bottle
and hope, but I've
no idea what'll
happen
next

***Geoff Lowe***

## WHO AND WHERE

Here I stand at the water's edge
I'm lost and all at sea
My own heart a distress signal
Please, O please rescue me.

How I came to be here
Oh where - I cannot tell
All I see is rocks
And relentless sea swell.

I'm sure - I hope I have a loved one
Because I have an emptiness and pain
Whoever they are I need them
And long to be with them again

In the hope you read this message
In a bottle pass it on will you
I wish all a safe successful journey
My love and gratitude is true

***Ann Weavers***

## No Goodbyes

You filled my eyes with tears, you filled my heart with woe
You left me broken-hearted, you didn't have to go
You took your life so precious, felt nothing else there was to give
No longer could you take the pain, no longer could you live
But life's a gift to treasure, the greatest gift of all
So live it to the most before taking one last fall
From the wonder of life's colours, to the very air we breathe
When given the gift of life it's not our choice to leave
I'll leave my fate to God, I think that way is best
For he'll know why it's time to die and so lay me down to rest
Though I feel you here in spirit your presence is sadly missed
My farewells left unsaid, my goodbyes left unkissed
But wherever you are now, I hope it's peace you'll find
And I pray a peace will come one day to those you left behind.

***Jacqueline Rands***

## A Message In A Bottle

'Dear friend, should you find this message afloat
Don't rush to my rescue by ship or by boat,
I'm happier away from sad 'civilisation',
Castaways come here by God's invitation.
I've no need for TV, for gas or pollution,
In nature's own lap I've found my solution.
The island is lovely, not too populated,
And I with my girl am happily mated.
We live in a hut all covered with thatch
And the gorgeous sunsets are a wonder to watch,
I fish for my dinner, with fruit in excess,
With breezes so balmy, like a lover's caress,
The swimming's just great, with waters sky-blue,
Who'd want to be rescued? I wouldn't, would you?
I've lost excess weight, I'm now supple and slim,
Whereas your lifestyle is hectic and grim.

Who needs to be 'rescued', who needs to be 'saved'?
Perhaps it is you, when true living is craved,
So let me be happy, just pass on your way,
While you suffer and stress, I sing and I play.
For reasons quite obvious, I shan't give my address,
Leave me to contentment, you keep your distress.

***Emmanuel Petrakis***

## ISOLATED

Lost, alone, rejected here
My desert island's full of fear.
There is no welcome home for me,
And all around seems endless sea.
I trek across the boundless sand,
My footprints mark uncharted land.
And as I watch the waves I think
Of the fresh streams I long to drink.
In my despair cry more salt tears,
That flow from all my waves of fears.
But as I see the clouds above,
I think of your much higher love.
I am reminded of your word -
Which says my cry is always heard.
My tears are in your 'bottle' kept
From every time I've ever wept,
So you will surely hear this call,
Pick up my 'message' as they fall,
Forming new patterns in the sand,
As I wait in this barren land.
Yet this despair's not dark to you,
You truly know me through and through.
There's nowhere I can hide from you
Even if I wanted to.
I scoop a handful of soft sand,
The grains run swiftly through my hand.
Could I count each grain of this shore,
Your thoughts of me are even more.
You meet me at my point of need
I find you here as God indeed!

*Lydia Lyrics*

## SOS For Help

I am shipwrecked on an island
  With scarcely any food
So I'm sending out this note for help
  In the hope it's understood

I only have a bottle
  In which to send my note
I hope it will find somebody
  Who can read what I have wrote

It is a small and rocky island
  With growth few and far between
With no human habitation
  And not an animal to be seen

I am hoping that the note I sent
  Is picked up rather fast
As any food I have to eat
  Will not have long to last

Being young I hope it's not the end
  Of human life for me
With newspapers saying 'A body's found
  In a lone island in the sea'.

***Lachlan Taylor***

## Remember Me

Dear John,
Remember me,
When I went to sea,
The hopes I had,
Life's so sad.
No dreams left now,
I'm not sure how, the last day will be,
But please, remember me.
Dear John.

***J Miles***

## Save My Soul

Being a cast away
Deep down in my soul,
I had no one to care for me
I could not find a way to go.

Lost in my own little world
Who could come to rescue me,
My plight was bad,
For no way out could I see.

I needed the fruit of the spirit
I needed forgiveness inside,
Lord have you a message
For me? This I cried.

Am I special at all to you?
Will you cast away all of my sin?
Will you care for me
And rescue me within?

I crave for your help Lord
I'm longing to be saved,
I come to you only
Bless me and lift me from my morbid grave.

***Marion Staddon***

## UNDERCOVER AGENT

I found a bottle on the beach, a letter was inside,
And when I read the message, my eyes were open wide.
It said I am a prisoner, on the ship Saint Clair.
I am an undercover agent, but my cover has been laid bare.
I was on a drugs bust, but someone turned me in,
Now I am in trouble and the torture will soon begin.
Please tell my wife I love her, and my children too,
There is a telephone number now the rest is up to you.

***Don Goodwin***

## Message In A Bottle

To my dearest darling husband
As I write this with a shaking hand
I can't believe that I'm sitting
On a beach of golden sand.
At least it's a whole lot better
Than being tossed above the waves,
I haven't seen or heard the others
God bless their watery graves.
Oh I know you said I was foolish
To go out on such a craft
And we should have listened to the weather
It really was just daft.
So now I'm alone on an island
And I'm trying hard not to cry
For it looks like it's totally up to me
If I live or if I die.
Well I've made a sort of shelter
Found water fit to drink
I've even found some fruit to eat
So I'm doing okay, I think.
The weather is warm and sunny
I'm getting an all-over tan
Actually the only thing that I'm missing
Is the company of a man!
But it looks like my worries are over
For coming out from the tall palm trees
Is a beautiful dusky native boy
Long hair blowing in the breeze!
So dearest darling husband
I'm now feeling a whole lot better
And if this bottle should reach you
You may disregard this letter!

***Val Baker***

## MESSAGE IN A BOTTLE

I wondered, was I dreaming,
Or could it really be,
As I felt the soft and golden sand,
While looking out to sea.

I thought I was in paradise,
But no one else was there,
So I soon began to panic,
And spent some time in prayer.

Days, ages even weeks have passed,
And no one yet in sight.
I waved my arms and jumped about,
And yelled with all my might.

All hope had gone, I was sure to die,
What could I do but sit and write,
Please rescue me, please come and try,
And take me from this awful plight.

I placed my message in a bottle,
Off it went upon the sea,
And after many days I saw,
A rescue team searching for me.

Oh what a miracle took place,
It seems just too good to be true.
And yet I know that up above,
God watches over me and you.

***Ruth Lyttle***

## A Message In A Bottle

Here am I, stuck in the sand
With one corked bottle,
And pencil in hand,
I shall put on this paper,
Some words sent from me,
Then place it in the bottle,
And throw out to sea,
If you come to save me,
Please will you be good,
Remember to bring with you,
A morsel of food,
Like a sandwich, sweet biscuit,
But the best thing would be
A hot, piping hot, strong cup of tea.

***V V Oliver***

## A Message In A Bottle

No playboy's pleasure ground, this,
But a bare haven
For the encircling seas of a life.
Here be no faeries gentle
Nor monsters either -
Only the whispering spirits
Of abandoned others
To greet me.

The ground grows cold now
As the sun sinks low.
I no longer search
For food, drink or comfort.
These, together with love
And joy and peace
I have known in abundance.
Now I can relinquish all,
Staying only to send to the world
Through whoever may find it
This, my credo:

Life is for living and loving
And ultimately for leaving
Without grieving.
Placed in the bottle of my memories
I launch it with my blessing.

***J L Sealey***

## AM I REALLY ME

My bottle holds a story,
Of what I really am,
Most of me is water,
The rest six foot of spam.

I sit here on this piece of rock,
Surveying nothing much,
I only saw myself today,
Whilst limping with my crutch.

I hope that shark out there is well,
But I will not swim near,
'Cause honestly I cannot swim,
So I am just stuck here.

One day I saw a mirage,
Or did I? I don't know,
Perhaps you think that I've gone mad,
That's what they'll say, you know.

So if you ever spot me,
I don't know what you'll find,
The spam will have been eaten,
And the water's turned to brine.

In fact, perhaps I never was,
You'll really never know,
So this message in a bottle,
Deserves a kick from your right toe.

***John Cook***

## Hopes Abandoned

That mountain never did get scaled
Nor fish reeled on a hook
That poem never was regaled
Nor yet have written book.

Hot air balloon in summer sky
Held not my fearful frame
Big prize from *Ernie* passed me by
He quite forgot my name.

No brave attempt at channel swim
Nor glider took, to flight
The eyes once young are now too dim
For ghostbusting at night.

I never climbed the apple tree
Nor jumped the gate beyond
Was not at Ritz for dainty tea
Or skated frozen pond.

I never tally-ho'd with hunt
Nor danced like Fred Astaire
Cruised not the Cam in student punt
Or went to Scarborough Fair.

So many dreams are unfulfilled
Not least the search for mate
And when he came, alas for me
It was too late, too late.

My hopes now dwell on next time round
Perchance I'll have that pleasure
For very soon I go to ground
A buried unclaimed treasure.

***Marion P Webb***

## MESSAGE IN A BOTTLE

Well, bread and butter,
Never appealed to me much in life,
But even a dry crust, would taste like a gammon steak,
If now I had one, on which to bite.

A pint of beer, is out of the question,
In fact, any drink is at all,
Though I'm surrounded by water,
For a sore throat, as a cure is all that is might be useful for.

I've never had a love of umbrellas,
But I'm thankful I've got one, though really it's a palm tree,
And it's multi-purpose in helping to stop the rain,
And keep out the sun's heat.

And that's about it,
All that I own, apart from my clothes,
And the sandcastles that I've built,
That are the closest, I've got to a home.

So in this bottle, I'm putting my trust,
With this message inside -
That 'hope' may find it, and come to my rescue,
Before 'death' does arrive.

***Bakewell Burt***

## Sun-Drenched Solitude?

I might pass the time
Like a child the ice-cream van,
A look and a lick.

Vanilla for memories
With its constant spillage
Of frost and candyfloss

On the surrounds of paradise?

***Marylène Walker***

## Mermaids

The sea hitting the rocks
so wild and untame
the sound of the mermaid
singing on the rocks of love
and loneless,
with her long beautiful
hair and her blue, gray
and green tail, her beautiful
full breasts a passion to all
men who see her and fall
in love but will die by
the sea.

***Olive Irwin***

## EBB TIDE

The words I tried to utter,
Were drowned in rainy gutters.
How could you recognise this fella?
Your eyes masked by black umbrella
There was only one more sin
Squelch out, where once I squelched in.

***K M Jeffery***

## FIDELITY

Do you think that I could stay from you,
And never more be by your side.
Then ask the sun no more to shine,
And her light forever hide.

Do you think that I could stay from you;
Then ask the sea why it returns;
To crash upon the lonely shore,
Like lovers' hearts break evermore.

And could I ever be from you,
Then ask the moon and stars above,
Why they so love the Milky Way,
And then you'll know why I should stay.

***Windsor Hopkins***

## REFLECTION

If this gets through
Washed up on a shore
Please let out its contents
So I can close the past's door.

It's a return into time
To tell of mistakes I have made
I'm trapped in this place
With not much shade.

Nothing but time
To reflect on one's life
Of goodness and badness
And sometimes strife.

To all those souls
I may have upset
Please send forgiveness
So my ghosts, I can forget.

It's strange really
Just reflecting on your past
But nothing else to do
These thoughts will last.

How I got here
I don't quite know
If God gives me a chance
I will get up and go.

Maybe I'm here
To put right what I've done wrong
To receive their forgiveness
And turn sadness to song.

***Rob Passmore***

## Fin De Siécle Island
## *Or*
## Desert Island Tsks!

My dearest world, to you I write
Without hint of *mal-de-mer,*
Concerning of, in troth, my plight
Upon this island fair.

No home, no friends, no books, no games,
No gentle summer rain;
My savage breast, no music tames,
Nor none can I obtain.

No Shakespeare, Bible, or fave discs;
Sue Lawley got it wrong.
The only show this climate risks
Is *'Going For A Thong'*.

Just endless searing sunshine, and
A scorched sky, like a griddle;
An infinity of sea and sand,
And me slap in the middle.

No neighbours, noise, no cars, no gripes,
No work, no mobile phones,
No complex inter-relationshipes,
Just me, and me alone.

A Croesus of quiet solitude
On a contemplative throne,
Whose bleached sandcastle walls eschewed
The kingdoms he'd once known.

And so, I bid you all, *Adieu!*
But, verily, don't weep it;
Horizons hide your world from view,
And that's how I aim to keep it.

*The Beginning*

***David H Woods***

## ENOUGH SAID!

A message in a bottle
I threw it in the sea
It uplifted my spirits
Between you and me.

'Dear mother-in-law
I have a story to tell you
Of my weeping and crying
On hearing what befell you.

Now you're in a hospital bed
With your leg stretched high above your head
I visualise your pained expression
Your demands and claims of deep depression.

No, I did not leave those gardening boots so you would trip
Despite your constant bickering lip
My plan was to mow your lawn
How did I know you would trip and fall?

This bottle is carrying my mirth away
Now I know you're coming to stay
A high price for one careless act
You always win, that's a fact.

Welcome mother-in-law - *do* take our bed
My favourite seat and papers unread.'

I know I'll be paying for this mishap for life
'Cause I'm madly in love with my trouble and strife!

***Gloria Hargreaves***

## UNTOLD LOVE

I love the warmth of your
arms about me. The soft
whisperings of love you betray.
How can I not adore you
when your love is shown this way.

As darkness falls and we're
apart, I miss you most of all.
And hope that when to rest
I go, sleep will fast befall.

For I wish the day to come
when you I'll see once more
so then I can but tell you
it is you that I adore.

***Beryl Smyter***

## PLEASE HELP ME

I am on this remote island,
  Without a radio or phone,
So I'm glad you've found my message
  Cos I'm out here, all alone.

I thought my life was over,
  As my boat began to sink,
Because tho' I'm safe on this island,
  I need food and fresh water to drink.

So I've drawn a map on this letter,
  For you to follow and rescue me,
From this bare, rocky island,
  And this cruel, angry sea.

Now I'm glad this bottle containing my message,
  Was also washed up here,
For the thought of never being rescued,
  Is my greatest fear.

***Jean Hendrie***

## To Whom It May Concern

To whom it may concern
Please help to rescue me
Shipwrecked on this island
I was washed up by the sea.

The days are hot and lonely
At night the cold sets in
How I miss my cosy bed
And cuddling up to kin.

I'm longing for a nice hot bath
And a steaming mug of tea
Buttered crumpets, cheese on toast
Are memories now for me.

I'm living on just coconuts
There's a plentiful supply
If I don't get off this island soon
I fear that I will die.

In this bottle is a map
The island's clear to see
If you should find this message
Please come to rescue me.

***Susan May Downs***

## ALONE!

Far removed from mankind - I find myself alone
I do find at this time - I have lowest thoughts coming into my mind.
I do have a real need to be forgiven - for the things I said in haste,
That were meant to harm - the very living soul - and things
I did in a selfish way. That I in time should gain.
Proving at this time I can never come face to face -
and from words spoken, tell them how I feel, hold my hands out
in a friendly way. Now at this late hour - I must trust in the one
I can't see - understanding one that dwells alone - is not wise - amen.

***Rowland Patrick Scannell***

## UNTITLED

Surrounded by the clear blue sea,
can someone help? Please read my plea!
I woke up lying on the sand,
I'm stranded on this barren land.
All that's left from on the ship,
a bottle, pen and paper strip,
the sea and wind blew the ship apart,
I don't have a clue of where to start.
I need some water and some food,
before I'm taken from this earth for good,
no one is left, they must have drowned,
from when the ship did run aground.
The captain sent an SOS,
come help me please I'm in a mess,
as I lay me down to rest,
I pray my bottle does its best!

***Margaret Davies***

## Struggle To Satisfy

Life is a powerful force,
Love, friendship and affection,
Hatred, killing and war.

To fulfil the fullness,
And soothe the salvaged,
We first need to look and listen.

Anger, fear and foolishness,
For all that lives and parts us,
We shall continue the fight for life!

***D A Young***

## A Message In A Bottle

Please come and get me
Whoever you may be,
I'm stuck on this island
Surrounded by sea.

I fell from a ship
And washed up on this shore
My body all bruised and battered
And sore.

There isn't much food
Though bananas are rife
I can't eat bananas
For the rest of my life.

I have water to drink
From a freshwater lake
But I long for a coffee
And a piece of cream cake.

I'm tired and bored
With sand in my toes
It gets in my ears
My eyes and my nose.

I talk to myself
Throughout the long day
But I really don't seem
To have that much to say.

Wait! I see a young man
Quite scantily clad
Perhaps life on this island
Isn't so bad.

PS: Please ignore this message.

***Francine Perkins***

## CATCH ME QUICK

Catch me quick, I leave today,
No way to stop me, I'm on my way,
To try and find that Crock of Gold,
At the rainbow's end, or so I'm told,
Just like a bird that's in full flight,
Soaring high just like a kite,
If you bind me 'round the ties I'll break,
You for granted, I'd never take,
Catch me quick before the dawn,
Not with eyes on me to scorn,
No way to stop the turning tide,
Gone forever, from you I hide.

***W Curran***

## SINGLE MALT

If you find this poem
From this single whisky bottle
Then you may know the plight
Of this drunken island dweller.
From falling from an aeroplane
To my shute ripping on a bird
Falling in sharpened stinging bushes
And bathing in piranha infested waters
To eating ants for lunch.
I wouldn't say I'm lonely
As the wildlife is game
But the gym's preferable
To escaping lions each and every day.
If you can assist
My island is quite small
It's surrounded by blue waters
And has sand upon its shores.

***John Holdsworth***

## Last Words

In heat of sun I seek the word
Which best can tell you what occurred . . .
I fell from deck of passing ship,
No one to watch if I should slip,
And dashing sea set me ashore
On desert island; now no more
For comfort, can I clasp your hand.
Unless this bottle reach the land
And bring my message; then I cry
To you, dear friend, my last goodbye.

If rescuers should cross the wave,
Fresh water, crusty bread I'd crave,
Apples to speak of autumn's gift,
But, best of all, your words to lift
My aching heart where sorrows live
With that sweet magic, 'I forgive.'
No evil deeds our lives divide,
Just careless word, or thoughtless pride,
But still they sting: forgive them, friend,
That I shall rest, when life shall end,
Upon the joyous certainty,
Your changeless love will comfort me.

***Kathleen M Hatton***

## MY LITTLE BOTTLE

The sea was like a mill pond
as I set sail for distant lands.
My dream of palms and coconuts,
stood gay upon golden sands.

My yacht the Sunflower Queen,
shall surely get me there,
her hull of gleaming mahogany,
with proud sails kissing the air.

For some reason the sea showed anger,
and tossed us both around,
near to an abandoned inlet,
my Queen sadly ran aground.

Now I sit alone here, my Queen has
vanished from sight.
My only possessions, a soggy biro,
and a paper bag on which to write.

How long have I been here?
Only the sun portrays passing time.
Seems a decade and a day,
since the ocean commit its crime.

Today I found a bottle,
floating on a woodland pond,
so in it I've placed a message,
in hope you'll soon respond.

So that is how I got there,
I recalled to Captain Scott,
in charge of the rescuing schooner,
*and* my little bottle that I forgot.

***Steve Kettlewell***

## Devil's Cove

Lonely pebbled beach
clambered cliff surround
defying rescued reach
softly spirit bound
stretching barren sky
scattered rigging rope
deafened drowning sigh
starving mustered hope
soaking splintered pyre
abandon sputtered smoke
denying flickered fire
stoic silence broke
crying salted tear
eerie quietened cave
battling morbid fear
weaving watching wave
darkened dismal dank
boiling angered froth
piling fragment plank
ripping ragged cloth
flapping tattered sail
wetly clinging weed
final hammered nail
fighting urgent need
cutting razored rock
waiting timeless tide
echoing muffled mock
final watered ride.

***Paul Birkitt***

## MESSAGE IN A BOTTLE

Mighty sea take me within your unrelenting folds
And take me on a journey to some distant land
And put me down upon a coral shore where I
Shall be opened by the tender hand of a dusky maiden.

For I was cast into the sea by a lonely soul who wished
Only to find a place with a different outlook on
Life where there is peace and tranquillity amongst
A peaceful race of people who are at peace with themselves!

If I am captured in the net of some fisherman or
Discovered in the belly of a great fish set me adrift
Once more and let me find the place to where my
Sender hopes to find a new way of life.

I wonder if this message in bottle shall
With your ebb and flow find a sandy
Beach on which this scrap of paper shall be found
Or tossed away without regard.

***Derek J Morgan***

## INFORMATION

We hope you have enjoyed reading this book - and that you will continue to enjoy it in the coming years.

If you like reading and writing poetry drop us a line, or give us a call, and we'll send you a free information pack.

Write to :-

**Triumph House Information**
**Remus House**
**Coltsfoot Drive**
**Peterborough**
**PE2 9JX**
**(01733) 898102**